REDEMPTION SONG

The Promise of American Diversity:
Values for the 21ˢᵗ Century

ROBERT L. LATTIMER

PAGE PUBLISHING, INC.
Conneaut Lake, PA

First originally published by Page Publishing 2021

ISBN 978-1-6624-1834-1 (hc)
ISBN 978-1-6624-1833-4 (digital)

Printed in the United States of America

A people that values its privileges above its principles soon loses both.

—Dwight D. Eisenhower

This book is dedicated to the following:

Dr. R. Roosevelt Thomas Jr., who was the founder and president of the American Institute for Managing Diversity Inc., located at Morehouse College, is the author of more than seven books on the topic of diversity, who spent thousands of hours providing me his wisdom. He was a special intellectual gift to me and to so many others; Dr. Thomas was a true professional, and I respected him greatly.

Professor Lucy Taksa, PhD, is professor of management and the director of Centre for Workforce Futures, at Macquarie University Business School—Sydney, Australia, whereupon there were many working collaborations between the two of us (far too few, I must say) involving Rutgers University, Macquarie University, the University of Paris at Dauphine, and the Martin Luther King Center at Atlanta, Georgia. Lucy, to learn from you is a growth experience; you are a true professional.

Larry Baytos, formally executive vice president at the Quaker Oaks Company, was most often referred to as the "honest broker" who had the strategic vision and relationship skills to connect Dr. Thomas's consulting group with one of the world's most respected consulting firms, Towers Perrin, thus providing a win-win situation within the world of the competitive marketplace; thank you, Larry, for your strategic skills and, of course, for your friendship.

Rollie Stichweh, the managing partner at Towers Perrin, recognizing the marketplace's competitive advantage to provide the Towers Perrin firm a profit and to help make the world a better place, upon Larry Baytos's counsel, and at his and my leadership, acquired Dr. Thomas's consulting organization, and as they say, the rest is history. Being supported by the vast resources at Towers Perrin, the diversity consulting practice became the world's largest in terms of the number of clients, size of the practice, and applied research conducted. Thank you, Rollie, for valuing diversity at so many levels.

Thabo Mbeki, the second president of the truly free and democratic Republic of South Africa, following the presidency of Nelson Mandela, you and Tamsanqa Max Maisela, executive chairman of the South African Post Office and Post Bank, were men of the highest integrity and vision and true examples of excellence in public service. It was a pleasure working with both of you; thank you for the opportunity.

Judith Griffey, a former partner at Towers Perrin consulting, a person of integrity, and a highly talented and skilled executive-level consultant with boardroom presence, was the first person that I hired from within Towers Perrin to provide additional leadership for the global diversity consulting practice which I led. Judith always had my back. I can never thank Judith enough for her many contributions; thank you, Judith, for always being a true professional.

Carl Van Horn, distinguished professor of Public Policy at the Edward J. Bloustein School of Planning and Public Policy and director at the John J. Heldrich Center for Workforce Development at Rutgers, The State University of New Jersey, had the vision to establish the Office of Diversity Studies, within the Heldrich Center, for which I was appointed the scholar. Our renowned annual symposiums, the State of Workforce Diversity, had become the leading international symposium for the presentation of the leading research and trends regarding the topic of diversity; thank you, Carl, for our collaborative and leading edge work.

CONTENTS

FOREWORD

I have found it to be a rich discussion what the Swedish economist Gunnar Myrdal, writing in 1944, and presented by Jon Meacham in his book, *The Soul of America*, the battle for our better angels, called the American Creed: "A devotion to the principles of liberty, of self-government, and of equal opportunity for all regardless of race, gender, religion, or nation of origin. The genius of America lies in its capacity to forge a single nation from peoples of remarkably diverse racial, religious, and ethnic origins; the American Creed envisages a nation composed of individuals making their own choices and accountable to themselves, it is what all Americans should learn, because it is what binds all Americans together."

In Robert Lattimer's *The Promise of American Diversity: New Values for the Twenty-First Century*, he reaffirms the beauty of American diversity within the American context and the need to recapture that essence, which made America truly a great country, though not a perfect one. Robert's concept of American diversity rest solidly within the values of liberty, freedom, opportunity, justice, and economic equality.

11

Diversity today encompasses people from every corner of the globe with varying cultures, languages, and religions. It encompasses both genders, spans the entire age spectrum; it is that spectrum that made America great, not the need to be so.

My life and that of my parents and three sisters are but one example of the personification of the American story—a story that Robert is framing through the lens of the twenty-first century, that represents the promise of American diversity and its future, by resetting old values to new ones, which is my story and that of so many others, different but similar to me.

My parents, my three sisters, and I were born in South Korea, not the ultra-modern South Korea of today, and we struggled economically upon immigrating to America in 1976; I was thirteen years of age and five feet, one inch tall, yet we were fortunate.

Before coming to America, I imagined so many things, so many wonderful things about this place. I had good dreams, but mostly, I read a lot about America and of its opportunities, things one could do, big cities, supermarkets, and the like. I did what most Korean kids do—I studied, and my sisters did the same. I even remember, to this day, reading an article in *Time Magazine* describing Asian Americans as "the model minority." I now know what that meant then, to assimilate!

Once in America, and completing my high school with a grade point average of 3.4 out of a possible 4.0, I decided to stay close to home, to support the wishes of my parents as I considered what college to attend, and as a result, I graduated with a bachelor of science degree in chemical engineering from Manhattan College and continued my studies completing a master of science degree in environmental engineering.

After college, I entered the corporate world working for some of America's best-known companies, such as Colgate Palmolive, Johnson & Johnson, and currently Teva Pharmaceutical, now at the senior director level, and although the work has been demanding, it has also been rewarding.

Yet there is one thing that I have noticed as I travel internationally and within the United States; we are no longer united as a country. We no longer have that unity that my parents, my sisters, and I noticed when we arrived in America. We seem to have lost "that loving feeling," the spirit of diversity and its importance, the valuable role that diversity has played at making America the most desired place to come from faraway places.

Robert's book offers us a rich account of America's struggle with the division in our immigrant nation and a historical summary of its once-enslaved people. And as true to form, he offers us meaningful solutions for our future.

ROBERT L. LATTIMER

This is a timely book that I recommend.

Ann Lee-Jeffs
Senior Director
Environment and Product Stewardship
Teva Pharmaceutical Inc.

PREFACE

The beauty of American diversity is that it promises to be inclusive within the human context, it promises to celebrate our differences and that of our similarities, it unleashes enormous potential within all sectors of society, it draws on the contributions of all Americans to ensure that our representative and participative democratic process is as it was established in the Declaration of Independence: "We hold these truths to be self-evident, that all men are created equal, that they are endowed by their Creator with certain unalienable Rights, that among these are Life, Liberty and the pursuit of Happiness."

My book will address what I consider to be one of the most sensitive issues that continue to confront America, and that is our values and ideals as twenty-first-century Americans.

I will address these issues by first presenting what I consider to be the cultural roots or, shall I say, the stated values of America, as outlined in Jefferson's Declaration, as presented in the Constitution of the United States.

As such values were for but a few when written; though more aspiration when written at the time, yet African Americans fought to make them truly American.

As Nikole Hannah-Jones, a researcher, staff writer, and the driving force of the 1619 initiative at the *New York Times Magazine,* August 18, 2019, through her detail and important research, documented, "it was near Point Comfort that the British colony of Virginia, a ship carried 20 enslaved Africans, who were sold to the colonists. America was not America, but it was on its way of becoming so."

And as it was to be, colonial law quickly made a distinction between White indentured servants and that of the African slave and, in so doing, invented Whiteness in America as we now know it to be. I often, in my lectures at Rutgers and such, call this period of 1619 the cultural roots of American diversity, with all its complexity, tension, conflict, and social beauty.

It will also be my purpose to present my notion of the conceptual meaning of American diversity, with many of its implications, and how, in my mind, what makes this concept uniquely American, as American as George Washington, Thomas Jefferson, Abraham Lincoln, Lyndon Johnson, Dr. Martin Luther King Jr., Rosa Parks, and how it shaped America's first African American president, Barack Obama. And unlike other definitions of diversity, mine is rooted in America's African enslavement and how that enslavement of generations of a people has established the social culture of America.

I will also present the case for how the promise of American diversity, in this the twenty-first century, just might live up to American values as presented in 1776, for Americans of goodwill, even now, continue to struggle making this a more perfect union, union of how differences within my proposed American diversity context are strengths and not a weakness.

Based on my applied research of more than twenty years, I define American diversity as individual differences and similarities that is rooted in the African American enslavement; that's it, nothing more and nothing less. Yet in its simplicity, there are profound consequences that are making the most impact at establishing current public policy and, at safe guarding the future of our democracy.

As such, the functional concept of American diversity and its philosophical premise are represented in the first three lines of Abraham Lincoln's Gettysburg Address: "Fourscore and seven years ago, our fathers brought forth on this continent a new nation, conceived in liberty, freedom, and opportunity."

Thus, if we are to continue to apply the American experiment as I think that the framers of the Constitution had in mind, that is, in the absence of the enslaved African, and to include the equally of women, then we must continue to draw on what made us a great nation based on human sustainable values and principles, that valuing differences to ensure the strength of our nation could very well ensure the American future on truly inclusive terms.

I believe that my book addresses not only the soul of America but the essence of this unique and complex place of great promise for all in this the twenty-first century.

Robert L. Lattimer

ACKNOWLEDGMENTS

A number of individuals, organizations, and institutions have supported me in the writing of this book, and I would like to thank them all:

My children, Ebony, THope, Izzy, and Superson, who all represent intellectual and behavioral diversity; all have provided me encouragement throughout this project.

My colleagues at Rutgers, The State University of New Jersey, the John J. Heldrich Center for Workforce Development, and those within the Edward J. Bloustein School of Planning and Public Policy, where I conducted research, directed symposium, and lectured. Distinguished Professors Nancy DiTomaso and Hal Salzman and my teaching assistant, Dilafruz Nazarova, who listened to my ideas on diversity strategy and public policy, made many important contributions that enhanced my thinking and have responded by supporting my many forums and lectures on the topic of diversity, inclusion, global poverty, and public policy. This also included my colleagues at Harvard, University of California, and Professors Abbas Ali and Prashanth N. Bharadway, at Indiana University of Pennsylvania.

A special note of appreciation to Rutgers professor Ronald Quincy, who provided me his wisdom from his days as the chief operating officer at the Martin Luther King Center in Atlanta, Georgia, working for and with Mrs. Coretta Scott King, the widow of Dr. King, and that of his leadership as the chief operating officer of the Congressional Black Caucus; I have found Professor Quincy's insights to be of great value, to the extent that I encouraged his Rutgers hire.

Professor Jean-Francois Chanlat, at the University of Paris, Dauphine, where he convened an important symposium of the leading authorities on the topic of international perspectives regarding equality, diversity, and inclusion, because he was of the opinion that diversity is beyond borders.

Professor Chanlat was kind enough to include my expressions by having me author the concluding chapter, the epilogue in the symposium book published by Emerald, entitled "Management and Diversity: Thematic Approaches"; thank you, Professor Jean-Francois, for the opportunity to contribute.

Over the past several years, hundreds of executives have listened to my ideas by engaging my counsel, which included Bill Weldon, former Chairman/CEO at Johnson & Johnson, Anthony Carter of Johnson & Johnson; Howard Schultz of Starbucks Coffee Company; Hazel O'Leary, former United States secretary of energy; Herb Williams of ATT; Dr. Sidney Harris, former dean and professor of the J. Mack Robinson School of Business, Georgia State University; Mary Harris, PhD. scientist, Ayesha Krishnan Hamilton, Esq., Board of Directors, New Jersey State Bar Association; Bill Hackney and Jim Skesavage of Atlanta Capital Management; Jeremy Durham, executive director of the Boulder Housing Partners; Michael Rambert, Esq., General Counsel, Morehouse School of Medicine. Curtis Brown, former chief of staff to the chairman and chief operating officer at Merrill Lynch, Simone, and Ernest Gans of Gans Gans and Associates; Peter Yeung Distinguished Architect; Hattie Dorsey, founder and president, Atlanta Neighborhood Development Partnership Inc., Magdalena Yue, my executive assistant; Professor Mohale and Phuti Mahanyele of South Africa, Joe Lopez, United States Marine Corps—to name but a few.

A special recognition to Richard H. Mitchell, Harvard class of '75, and to Professor Marvin L. Winitsky, JD, PhD, who provided me substantial research data, insight, and advice regarding the metaphor "Sambos glasses."

I also thank all the diversity scholars that have and are continuing to do the all-important work, for I have truly benefited and have, to some degree, recognized and included your work within my work here. Please forgive me if I have not citied you as appropriate; it was not my intent to do so.

To Dr. Hassan Minor, most recently executive vice president at Howard University, who provided me important comment to the completion of this book.

And to my parents and grandfather Mariagnes E. Lattimer, PhD, James C. Lattimer, and Charles E. Minor, who worked far too hard in their attempt to provide me an equal opportunity in life.

To all these individuals, organizations, and institutions, I offer my profound respect and appreciation.

SONG I

The American Beginning 1619

As I would not be a slave, so
I would not be a master. This
expresses my idea of democracy.

—Abraham Lincoln

It is my belief that we must come to understand or,
at the very least, develop an awareness of what I call
the cultural roots of White racism in America, which
is at the very foundation of our democratic form of
government. And it is from that point, the beginning to where we are at present, that unique yet at
times that uncomfortable place that many of us find
us even today.

What follows is a summary description, an American history of sorts, of our experience with America's race dilemma, as uncomfortable as it may be for some, yet it's part of dealing with our, the American sickness, so that we may prescribe the right medicine, the right vaccine, for our collective cure.

So then, let us begin to understand America's cultural roots so that we may move on and establish a new value system that is based not on anyone's race but on how our differences and seminaries enable all of us to be better Americans, better citizens, and better human beings.

So as the story of America, according to the narrative enshrined in the American civic historical account goes: A great wilderness was gradually populated by waves of hardy immigrants fleeing the oppressions of the Old World to build a better life in the new one.

Throwing off subordination to a distant throne, they made a commonwealth, the first in history to be founded explicitly on the principles of self-government and that of political equality and Christian values.

Over 401 years, they worked and sometimes fought to ensure that their new nation, conceived of liberty and dedicated to the proposition that all men (not women or people of color), were created equal. And they succeeded in creating a nation on that premise.

A pretty story, and like most folk tales, this one tells a kind of truth. But the reality is more complicated and complex in more ways than one, more nationally painful, and ultimately, more heroic.

The story ignores the tragic dimension of one aspect of the American reality that is of that institution, you know, the tragic dimension of the American enslavement of African people, not immigrants, that dimension that challenges the moral values from which it has been proclaimed as the ethical foundation of our, the American system of freedom and liberty. With that said, not all American ancestors came here to escape tyranny; many were brought here to further tyranny and economic development. Not all crossed the ocean to better themselves and their families; many were forcibly carried here, their families torn apart, their social structures smashed, their languages suppressed, to labor without compensation for the benefit of their oppressors.

In August of 1619, just twelve years after the English settled Jamestown, Virginia, one year before the Puritans landed at Plymouth Rock and 157 years before the English colonists decided they wanted to form their own country, the Jamestown colonists bought 20 to 30 enslaved Africans from English pirates. The pirates had stolen them from a Portuguese slave ship that had forcibly taken them from what is now the country of Angola. Those men and women who came ashore on that August day were the beginning of American slavery. They were among the 12.5 million Africans who would be kidnapped from their homes and brought in chains across the Atlantic Ocean in the largest forced migration in human history. Almost two million did not survive the grueling journey known as the Middle Passage.

Those individuals and their descendants trans-
formed the lands to which they'd been brought into
some of the most successful colonies in the British
Empire.

Through backbreaking labor, they cleared the
land across the Southeast. They taught the colonists
to grow rice. They grew and picked the cotton that,
at the height of slavery, was the nation's most valuable commodity, accounting for half of all American
exports and about 66 percent of the world's supply.
They built the plantations of George Washington,
Thomas Jefferson, and James Madison, sprawling
properties that today attract thousands of visitors
from across the globe captivated by the history of the
world's greatest democracy.

They laid the foundations of the White House
and the Capitol building, even placing with their
hands the Statue of Freedom atop the Capitol dome.
They lugged the heavy wooden tracks of the railroads
that crisscrossed the South and that helped take the
cotton they picked to the Northern textile mills, fuel-
ing the Industrial Revolution.

They built vast fortunes for White people
North and South; at one time, the second-rich-
est man in the nation was a Rhode Island slave
trader. Profits from Black people's labor helped
the young nation pay off its war debts and
financed some of our most prestigious universities.

It was the relentless buying, selling, insuring, and financing of their bodies and the products of their labor that made Wall Street a thriving banking, insurance, and trading sector and New York City the financial capital of the world, then and of today.

But it would be historically inaccurate to reduce the contributions of the African American people to the vast material wealth created by bondage.

Black Americans have also been, and continue to be, foundational to the idea of American freedom. More than any other group in this country's history, we have served, generation after generation, in an overlooked but vital role: It is we who have been the perfecters of this democracy.

The United States is a nation founded on both an ideal and a misrepresentation. Our Declaration of Independence, signed on July 4, 1776, proclaims that "all men are created equal" and "endowed by their Creator with certain unalienable rights." But the White men who drafted those words did not believe them to be true for the hundreds of thousands of Black people in their midst.

"Life, liberty, and the pursuit of happiness" did not apply to fully one-fifth of the country's population at that time. Yet despite being denied the freedom and the justice, Black Americans believed in the American creed.

Through centuries of Black resistance and protest, we have helped the country live up to its founding ideals. And not only for ourselves, Black rights struggles paved the way for other movements for opportunities as well.

Without the idealistic, strenuous, and patriotic efforts of African Americans, our democracy today could most likely look very different from what we now have. So then, it could very well be known, given our American history, that the year 1619 is as important to the American story as 1776.

In June of 1776, Thomas Jefferson sat at his desk in a rented room in Philadelphia and wrote the following: "We hold these truths to be self-evident, that all men are created equal, that they are endowed by their Creator with certain unalienable Rights that among these are Life, Liberty and the pursuit of Happiness." Fore, the last 241 years of American history freedom and self-governance has defined our global reputation as a land of liberty, and if you worked hard enough and played by the rules, opportunity would be yours in this great land.

It is reported that as Jefferson composed his inspiring words, a teenage boy who would enjoy none of the rights, liberties, and freedoms, waited to serve at his master's call.

At the time, one-fifth of the population within the thirteen colonies struggled under a brutal system of slavery unlike anything that had existed in the world before or after. Chattel slavery was not conditional but racial.

It was heritable and permanent, not temporary, meaning generations of Black people were born into it and passed their enslaved status onto their children. Enslaved people were not recognized as human beings but as property that could be mortgaged, traded, bought, sold, used as collateral, given as a gift, and disposed of violently; there was never ever any kind of slavery like American slavery.

Jefferson's fellow White colonists knew that Black people were human beings, but they created a network of laws and customs, astounding for both their precision and cruelty, that ensured that enslaved people would never be treated as human.

As the abolitionist William Goodell wrote in 1853, "If anything founded on falsehood might be called a science, we might add the system of American slavery to the list of the strict sciences."

Enslaved people could not legally marry. They were barred from learning to read and restricted from meeting privately in groups. They had no claim to their own children, who could be bought, sold, and traded away from them on auction blocks alongside furniture and cattle or behind storefronts. Enslaved people could own nothing, will nothing, and inherit nothing.

One of many important dates of significance in the history of the African American was August 14, 1862, which was five years after the nation's highest courts declared that no Black person could be an American citizen (the *Dred Scott* case). President Abraham Lincoln called a group of five esteemed free Black men to the White House for a meeting.

It was one of the few times that Black people had ever been invited to the White House as guests. The Civil War had been going on for more than a year, and it was not going well for Lincoln and the North. Even Britain was contemplating whether to intervene on the side of the Confederacy, and Lincoln was forced to reconsider his opposition to allowing Black Americans to fight for their own liberation. The president was also weighing a proclamation that threatened to emancipate all enslaved people in the states that had seceded from the Union if the states did not end the rebellion. The proclamation would also allow the formerly enslaved to join the Union Army and fight against their former "masters." But Lincoln worried about what the consequences of this radical step would be. Like many White Americans, he opposed slavery as a cruel system at odds with American values and ideals, but he also opposed Black equality. He believed that free Black people were a "troublesome presence" incompatible with a democracy intended only for White people. "Free them, and make them politically and socially our equals?" Lincoln had said four years earlier. "My own feelings will not admit of this, and if mine would, we well know that those of the great mass of White people will not."

That August day, as the men arrived at the White House, they were greeted by the towering Lincoln and a man named James Mitchell, who, eight days before the meeting, had been given the title of a newly created position called the commissioner of emigration.

This was to be his first assignment. Historical records indicate that after exchanging a few niceties, Lincoln got right to the point.

He informed his guests that he had gotten Congress to appropriate funds to ship Black people, once freed, to another country.

"Why should they leave this country? This is, perhaps, the first question for proper consideration," Lincoln told them. "You and we are different races. Your race suffers very greatly, many of them, by living among us, while ours suffer from your presence. In a word, we suffer on each side." Todd Brewster goes into great detail of this in his book, *Lincoln's Gamble*, which he, Carl Van Horn, and I discussed at Rutgers a few years ago.

One can only imagine the heavy silence in that room, as the weight of what president Lincoln said momentarily stole the breath of these five Black men. It was 243 years to the month since the first of their ancestors had arrived on these shores, before even Lincoln's family, long before most of the White people insisting that this was not their country. The Union had not entered the war to end slavery but to keep the South from splitting off, yet Black men had signed up to fight. Enslaved people were fleeing their plantations, trying to join the effort, serving as spies, sabotaging confederates, taking up arms for his cause as well as their own. And now Lincoln was blaming them for the war.

"Although many men engaged on either side do not care for you one way or the other, without the institution of slavery and the colored race as a basis, the war could not have an existence," the president told them. "It is better for us both, therefore, to be separated."

As Lincoln closed the remarks, Edward Thomas, the delegation's chairman, informed the president that they would consult on his proposition. "Take your full time," Lincoln said. "No hurry at all." Hurry they did not; there was never a reply.

To live 250 years of enslavement, ninety years of Jim Crow, sixty years of separate but equal, and thirty-five years of state-sanctioned redlining, as Ta-Nehisi Coates has said, "until we reckon with the compounding moral debts of our ancestors, America will never be whole."

Slavery is called America's original sin, but how many of us truly understand the myriad ways it has shaped our lives and that of our country even of today?

It is my position that it is not sufficient for many Whites to currently state that such conditions are not of their making, and as such, they have no responsibility, nor should they bear no such burden, and to them, I say, Do you not accept the advantages? The privileges?

SONG 2

The State of Diversity during the Presidency of Trump

> We should judge a person by the content of their character.
>
> —Dr. Martin Luther King Jr.

As the veteran Republican operative Stuart Stevens writes in his forthcoming book, *It Was All a Lie*, race "has defined the modern Republican party" ever since Richard Nixon's Southern strategy.

Trump is the master at cynically proclaiming, "I am the least racist person there is anywhere in the world."

As Max Boot presents in his May 27, 2020, *Washington Post* article where he states that "not all Trump supporters are racist. But they are complicit in his racism," Boot goes further to state that his *Post* colleague Brian Klaas writes: "If you're more upset by an athlete kneeling on a sports field than at a police officer kneeling on a African American man's neck until he dies, then you are the problem."

More telling, or shall I say, more reveling, was the Amy Cooper Central Park incident, because it provides real behavior insights regarding American race culture.

Michele Norris, whom I respect greatly for balanced investigative reporting, in her May 28, 2020, Washington Post article entitled "How Amy Cooper and George Floyd Represent Two Versions of Racism that African Americans Face Every Day."

So here is my definitive summary from Michele Norris's article, keeping in mind that I am over lading American race culture and the state of diversity during the Trump presidency and how Michele Norris conveys that Amy Cooper, the queen, is found to have no retort.

As Michele states, "How refreshing it would have been if Amy Cooper has said, 'Yep, that was a pretty clear act of racism on my part,' instead of apologizing to that man and insisting that she was not really a racist."

As Michele asserts, Amy Cooper "knew that Christian Cooper, the African-American man who was out birding in New York Central Park, did not present a threat to her life. But she also knew she was threatening his life by weaponizing her tears and using the 911 system as a kind of concierge arsenal to summon what could have wound up being the opening act to George Floyd's death in Minneapolis later the same day."

As Michele further asserts, "these two storylines, the African man confronted by White fragility in Central Park and the African man confronted with police brutality and death in Minneapolis, will forever be in conversation with each other," as they should be, for both represent versions of the same kind of constant racism that flows through American life every single day, for African American men regardless of education, income, status, or the other factors of potential and level of achievement, for Christian Cooper was a graduate of Harvard, and Mr. Floyd was a hardworking truck driver.

As Michele further presents, "a lot of people are condemning Amy Cooper without interrogating the implicit bias in their own actions. Sometimes it is as subtle as clutching your purse a little closer when an African American steps into an elevator. Sometimes it is as overt as willfully overlooking the patterns in hiring and promotion decisions, mortgage applications, and property assessments that lead to a condition in which the median White adult who attends college has more than seven times more wealth than the median African American who attends college, and four times the wealth of a Latino with similar education."

In America, economic exclusion is the engine of inequality; I know, I taught the honors course at Rutgers, the Bloustein School of Public Policy.

So as Michele states in her important article, "race fatigue is a real thing, and I understand how it can all be exhausting. But unease is no excuse for pretending racism has gone away, not when the evidence of inequality is still staring us in the face, informed by our history, fueled by our social norms, fertilized by social media, and stoked by a political opportunist."

In the end of the ongoing experience, Mr. Floyd was murdered in Minneapolis, Christian Cooper, in the moment that mattered, Amy weaponized her privilege and her tears to imperil the life of an African American man; he was spared. But as Michele notes, "I take no comfort, because I know that inequality still flourishes precisely because there is a quiet brand of bias, fear, status, expectation and otherness that marches alongside us every day, impacting some, invisible to others, until it's captured on a cellphone and goes viral for all to see."

The fact is that Donald J. Trump has been obsessed with race most of his adult life, from his apartments being found guilty of discrimination by not renting to financially qualified African Americans, to his political rise being built on promulgating the lie that the nation's first Black president was not born in the United States, to describing Mexicans as "rapists and murders."

Trump went further by

- stating a federal judge hearing a case about Trump University was biased because of the Judge's Mexican heritage and, therefore, could not render a nonpartial ruling;
- calling Obama, who was editor in chief of the *Harvard Law Review* at the time, "a terrible student, terrible." And announced that Obama should present his grades;
- calling the Nazis and White supremacists in Charlottesville "very fine people";
- calling Congress person Maxine Waters a person of "low IQ";
- calling for "a total and complete shutdown of Muslims entering the United States," including refusing to readmit Muslim American citizens who were outside the country at the time;
- calling demonstrating African American football athletes "sons of bitches";
- calling, in June of 2016, by pointing to one meeting attendee: "Oh, look at my African American over there, look at him, as through neosurgeon Ben Carson was in the zoo."

Now much of this is old news. Trump was still elected president of the United States of America, and as of this writing, his approval rating among Republicans is about 79 percent, yet I say, "Character? What kind of character does this American president have?"

On April 9, 2019, the highly respected Pew Research Center released its research findings of "Social and Demographic Trends: Race in America 2019" report.

The study was conducted by Juliana Menasce Horowitz, Anna Brown, and Kiana Cox.

In summary, a majority of Americans say race relations in the United States are bad, and of those, about seven in ten say things are getting worse. Roughly two-thirds say it has become more common for people to express racist or racially insensitive views since Donald Trump was elected president.

The following are what I consider to be a few data points:

1. 58% or six in ten Americans say race relations in the United States are generally bad.
2. 71% of Blacks are considerably more likely than Whites to agree with bad.
3. 56% of Whites.
4. 60% of Hispanics express negative views about the state of race relations.
5. Roughly two-thirds say it has become common for people to express racist views since Donald Trump was elected.
6. 56% of Americans say Trump, after two years into his presidency, has made race relations worse.
7. 15% say the president has made progress toward improving race relations.

8. Of Blacks, Hispanics, and Asians say Trump has made race relations worse.

9. 49% of Whites believe that Trump has made race relations worse.

10. Despite their generally negative assessments of the current state of race relations, Americans tend to say that most racial and ethnic groups get along well with one another.

11. One in five Black adults say all or most Whites in the United States are prejudiced against Black people.

12. 59% of adults say that being White helps them advance in the United States at least a little.

13. 72% Asians agree.

14. 69% Blacks and Hispanics agree.

15. Of questions 18, 19, 20, slavery affects the situation of Black people in America.

16. Six in ten US adults believe slavery continues to have an impact on Black people's status in the United States. Many say the legacy of slavery affects the position of Black people in society today.

Given the April 9, 2019, findings of the Social and Demographic Trends by the Pew Research Center, the current climate for race relations within the United States during three years of the Trump presidential administration could be described as dangerously toxic.

As Fintan O'Toole of the *Irish Times* states in his article of April 25, 2020, "When Trump took office, the conventional wisdom in the United States was that the Republican Party and the broader framework of the US political institutions would prevent him from doing too much damage. But Trump's presidency is not an aberration, as he has at least eight more months in power, based on the summary findings of the above Pew Research Center, Trump will pump more hatred and falsehood, more death-wish defiance of reason and decency. The idea of the US as the world's leading nation, an idea that has shaped the past century, has all but evaporated."

I have also found it to be more then important to note that in Justin Gest's book, *The New Minority: White Working Class Politics in an Age of Immigration and Inequality*, he asserts that "working-class Whites feel not only voiceless, but also silenced, especially in matters involving race. The way they understood racism is different from the way many persons of color understand racism, for them, racism has become an instrument of silence. It is a way of invalidating people. By saying someone is a racist; it means they cease to matter. Don't listen to them."

So when Donald Trump preaches at his rallies, "I am your voice," he has tapped into the White working class to be heard, they are now being heard, and as such, Trump's attraction is not merely substantive, but it's more symbolic. It will take more than canceling a social program to shake their allegiance to President Trump.

As Fintan O'Toole further states, "Either way, it will be a long time before the rest of the world can imagine America being great again."

At various times over the past three and a half years, many of us have asked what would happen if President Trump truly went over the edge or if his behavior became so frightening that his unfitness for the most powerful position on earth could no longer be denied.

In 2016 Republicans said Trump would grow serious and sober once he was faced with the awesome responsibilities of the office. Yet if I were to now give Republicans truth serum, they'd say, of course he's unfit to be president. Of course he's corrupt, of course he's incompetent, and of course he's the most dishonest person ever to step into the Oval Office. But they would also say, we can live with that, because he means Republicans keep power, they get more conservative judges, and they get all the policies they favor.

So that's the devil's bargain; that's the choice the Republicans are making at the expense of our country.

SONG 3

Income Inequality, Race, and Education

None of us is as smart as all of us.

—A Japanese proverb

There is a debate currently regarding the factors that are impacting the lack of progress of the African American in American society, and much of the debate centers on the theme that if we could only educate and motivate the African American, all would be well. The race issue, inequality, all factors that are currently negatively causing the race divide would be solved, that we will finally achieve racial educational, economic, harmony, and social cohesion within America.

In my efforts to examine the issue of American diversity, racial harmony, and how we, as well-meaning Americans, seek to attain a kind of human sustainability through racial harmony, I took a look at the correlation regarding the issue of race, education, and social progress of the African American within modern American society.

Operating from the premise that men and women of all races are born with the same range of abilities, and given my limitation for exploring this most important issue, I called upon my friend and colleague at Rutgers, the John J. Heldrich Center for Workforce Development, William M. Rodgers III, professor of public policy and the chief economist at the Heldrich Center, to provide me data on the topic. I didn't have far to go, as his office was on the second floor and mine on the third floor of the Heldrich Center.

Prior to Rutgers, Bill served as the chief economist at the United States Department of Labor, and he received his PhD in economics from Harvard University. Most important regarding this topic, Bill and one of his colleagues at the Economic Policy Institute, Valerie Wilson, who received her PhD in economics from the University of North Carolina at Chapel Hill, had conducted a study and published a report of their findings on September 20, 2016, at which I will reference by citing their research findings from their report entitled "Black-White Wage Gaps Expand with Rising Wage Inequality."

What follows are some of Bill's and Dr. Wilson's findings from their research study entitled "Black-White Wage Gaps Expand with Rising Wage Inequality," September 20, 2016.

1. Black-White wage gaps are larger as of September 20, 2016, than they were in 1979.

2. As of 2015, White men with the same education, experience, metro status, and region of residence, Black men make 22.0 percent less, and Black women make 34.2 percent less. Black women earn 11.7 percent less than their White female counterparts.

"Though the African American experience is not monolithic, research reveals that changes in Black education levels or other observable factors are not the primary reason the gaps are growing. For example, just completing a bachelor's degree or more will not reduce the Black-White wage gap. The gaps have expanded most for college graduates. Black male college graduates (both those with just a college degree and those who have gone beyond college) newly entering the workforce started the 1980s with less than a 10 percent disadvantage relative to White college graduates but by 2014 similarly educated new entrants were at a roughly 18 percent deficit."

Bill and Dr. Wilson further state that "racial differences in college education continued to narrow after the year 2000, but their estimated gaps for college graduates indicate that just completing a bachelor's degree or more will not reduce the Black-White wage gap. Black college graduates have higher wages than African American high school graduates, but significant wage gaps between Black and White college graduates have grown and persisted."

Bill and Dr. Wilson continue by stating, "It is wrong that as a society we send a message that you must get a college degree to obtain economic security, yet even then you will experience a sizable earnings disadvantage. This erosion in opportunity started in the 1980s, but little has been done to address it."

Bill and Dr. Wilson offer a number of recommendations regarding how to address the Black-White wage gaps with similar college education achievement levels, and they are as follows:

A. Convene a high level summit to address why Black college graduates start their careers with a sizable earnings disadvantage.
B. Consistently enforce antidiscrimination laws in the hiring, promotion, and pay of women and minority workers.

C. Under the Equal Employment Opportunity Commission, work with experts to develop metropolitan area measures of discrimination that could be linked to individual records in the federal surveys so that researchers could directly assess the role that local area discrimination plays in the wage setting of African Americans and Whites.

D. Require the Federal Reserve to pursue monetary policy that targets full employment, with wage growth that matches productivity gains.

So then what does all this mean in terms of American social cohesion, racial harmony, and human sustainability?

In terms of American social cohesion and racial harmony, Black-White wage gaps with similar education levels but lacking similar levels of achievement, in human earning terms, will have a negative impact on the African American family structure. It continues to flow from centuries of discrimination, from which the African American male is robbed of his dignity to provide for his family. It is reported that less than half of all African American children reach the age of eighteen, having lived all their lives with both of their parents. And in America, like most of the world, the family is the cornerstone of society.

The African American female is robbed of the opportunity to achieve a meaningful career of her choice, and the broad society is denied factors that would support human sustainability on an equal opportunity wage-earning basis.

As President Lyndon Johnson presented at the now-famous 1965 Commencement Address at Howard University, "Freedom is the right to share, share fully and equally, in American society, to vote, to hold a job, to enter a public place, to go to school. It is the right to be treated in every part of our national life as a person equal in dignity and promise to all others."

President Johnson went further in his address, "But freedom is not enough. You do not wipe away the scars of centuries by saying: Now you are free to go where you want, and do as you desire, and choose the leaders you please."

As Bill and Dr. Wilson's report presents, the Black college wage gap was on average resulted in Whites earning 18 percent more than the Black college graduate of similar education and region of the country.

The report suggests that there are other factors than college education that are creating the wage gap between Black and White.

This, too, is not pleasant to look upon. But it must be faced by those who serious intent is to improve the life of all Americans, as now is the time to move beyond opportunity to achievement.

SONG 4

Sambo Glasses

"Caught Their Eyes"

—Jay-Z

Sambo Glasses

Going all the way back to the year 1619, near a place called, interestedly, Point Comfort, Virginia, it is said within many sectors of the African American community that we have been helping to bring comfort to White folks ever since we have been old enough to distinguish ourselves from White folks.

Of course America was not yet called America, but Africans were called Africans, and they arrived at Point Comfort, all twenty of them, enslaved, who were sold to the colonists to make White folks' lives better, richer, and more comfortable.

In the relative modern context: in the fields, in games, within classrooms, at lunch counters, restaurants, in business meetings, in all facets of American life, in instance after instance, talk after talk, time after time, African Americans have answered the questions of Whites and have made an effort to put Whites at ease.

Yet through all the reaching, bending, stretching, twisting, and turning, Whites still viewed African Americans through the lens of Sambo glasses, as those partially civilized semi-human beings.

As the saying goes, when Sambo glasses are at the top of the noses of White folks, African Americans are viewed as a variation of the age-old stereotype; underneath the veneer of being viewed as civilized, African Americans are perceived as latent warriors, potential criminals, mean and illiterate, or docile and jovial.

After four hundred years of achievement, in countless interactions, discussions, and of course, the forty-fourth president of the United States of America, African Americans have, at best, been able to convince enlighten Whites to lower Sambo glasses.

Some, enlighten White folks have lowered Sambo glasses enough to see African Americans for brief moments as human, but it is rare that Sambo glasses are removed for full acceptance.

SONG 5

American Values, Going Onward

> Our human compassion binds
> us the one to the other as human
> beings who have learnt how to
> turn our hope for the future.
>
> —Nelson Mandela

The founders knew that the nation they were forming was an experiment, a test of the idea that people could live together and rule themselves, guided by the spirit of cooperation. The Constitution they devised was itself hammered out among those willing to compromise, thus giving birth to this experiment.

Upon being elected the first US president, George Washington, at his inauguration, said, "The preservation of the sacred fire of liberty and the destiny of the republican model of government are justly considered as deeply, perhaps as finally staked, on the experiment entrusted to the hands of the American people." It was a concept, and it was not inclusive; that was then!

In his wisdom and humility, Washington, I believe, saw the daunting challenge of keeping our experiment alive and the role of American citizens in proving to the world that people didn't need a king or a tyrant: We, the people, could rule ourselves.

Those included the Union soldiers who gave their last breath to hold the nation together and cast out the heinous practice of slavery that had been a defect since this nation's birth.

American values have not been just grounded on the founding concepts of liberty, freedom, and that of a representative democracy, for from some of its darkest hours, the United States has emerged stronger because of what I call values based on resilience.

And this American system of resilient values has not been in theory; it has been grounded in practice and in action. For between May and July of 1862, even as Confederate victories in Virginia raised doubts about the future of the Union, the American Congress and President Lincoln kept their eyes on the horizon, by enacting three landmark laws that shaped the nation's future:

The Homestead Act, which allowed Western settlers to claim 160 acres of public land apiece; the Morrill Act, which provided land grants for states to fund universities; and the Pacific Railway Act, which underwrote the transcontinental railroad.

Nearly seventy-five years later, in the depths of the Great Depression, with jobs in short supply and many Americans reduced to waiting in bread lines, President Franklin Roosevelt proved similarly farsighted. He concluded the best way to revive and sustain prosperity was not merely to pump money into the economy but to rewrite the rules of the marketplace, to reimagine the marketplace. "Liberty," Roosevelt said at the Democratic Party's convention in 1936, "requires opportunity to make a living, a living decent according to the standard of the time, a living which gives man not only enough to live by, but something to live for." His administration, working with Congress, enshrined the right of workers to bargain collectively, imposed strict rules and regulators on the financial industry, and created Social Security to provide pensions for the elderly and disabled.

Over the past half century, the fabric of American democracy has been stretched thin. The nation has countenanced debilitating decay in its public institutions and a concentration of economic power not seen since the 1920s. Many Americans live without financial security or opportunity; a relative handful of families holds much of the nation's wealth.

Over the past decade, the wealth of the top 1 percent of households has surpassed the combined wealth of the bottom 80 percent.

In a nation in which enduring racial inequalities in wealth and in health are reflected for those at the bottom, the chances of rising are in decline. By the time they reached thirty, more than 90 percent of Americans born in 1940 were earning more than their parents had earned at the same age. Yet those born in 1980, only half were earning more than their parents by the age of thirty; the erosion of the American dream is not a result of laziness.

These changes have become harder to reverse because the distribution of political power also is increasingly unequal. Our system of democracy is under strain as those with wealth increasingly shape the course of policymaking, acting from self-interest and perhaps also because it has become harder to imagine life on the other side of the divide as Joseph Stiglitz references in much of his work and as he presented before my class studying Global Poverty, in the fall of 2015 at the Edward J. Bloustein School of Planning and Public Policy at Rutgers.

"We have come to a clear realization of the fact that true individual liberty and freedom cannot exist without economic security and independence," so said Roosevelt to the nation in 1944.

The goal was never realized in full for all, but more importantly, since the late 1960s, the federal government has largely abandoned the attempt. The defining trend in American public policy has been to diminish government's role as a guarantor of personal liberty for all, one of America's core values demises.

One profound example is clear: During this period, executive pay has skyrocketed, and shareholders have enjoyed rising stock prices, at least until recently, while most workers are falling behind. If individual income had kept pace say, with the overall economic growth since 1970, Americans in the bottom 90 percent of the income distribution would be making an additional $12,000 per year, on average.

In effect, the current projected increase in inequality means every worker in the bottom 90 percent of the income distribution is sending an annual check for $12,000 to a member in the top 10 percent.

We Americans need to recover the optimism that has so often lighted the path forward.

Once as a young Marine, I learned that the crucible of a crisis provides the opportunity to forge ahead, in this case, to create a better society, within the values of our founders, yet the crisis itself does not do the work. Crises expose problems, but they do not supply the alternatives, let alone the political competence and will. Change requires ideas and leadership.

Nations often pass through the enormous crises, either unable to imagine a different path or unwilling to walk it; I know given my in-depth working relationship with Tamsanqa Max Maisela and others that represented the very fine leadership within South Africa that was responsible for leading the transformation and reconstruction of the country.

Americans had every reason to be concerned of President James Buchanan's ability to lead the nation through a civil war, or of President Herbert Hoover's ability to lead the nation out of the Great Depression, or of Wilson, Nixon, and Trump to address the crisis of their presidencies.

There is also a need for new ideas and for the revival of older ones, about what the government provides its citizens, its citizens provides its government, and what we as all Americans owe to one another; there is a need to currently establish trust and to have confidence in each other and in our institutions.

The larger issue is to increase the resilience of American society. This moment demands a restoration of the national commitment to a richer conception of freedom, as in equality of opportunity.

The purpose of the federal government, Lincoln once wrote to Congress on July 4, 1861, "to elevate the condition of men, to lift artificial burdens from all shoulders, and to give everyone an unfettered start and a fair chance in the race of life."

Lincoln's conception of "everyone" did not include everyone: It rested on the expropriation of Native American lands, and Lincoln's call was not inclusive, yet it was the beginning of the new way.

Roosevelt shared Lincoln's vision of government of sorts, but industry had replaced agriculture as the wellspring of prosperity, so he focused on ensuring a more equitable distribution of the nation's manufacturing output. And although slavery is called America's original sin, how many Americans truly understand the myriad ways it has shaped the lives of our country today? For although African Americans were treated as second-class citizens in many of Roosevelt's New Deal programs, Americans values and ideals are reshaping American culture as we now live by insuring that all Americans will have a stake in this the modern twenty-first century.

Many of us enjoy America's freedom by an accident of birth, yet we all live free in this land by our own choice. It is our responsibility to show respect and genuine friendship to one another as fellow citizens, including those with whom we sometimes disagree, by unifying around our radical idea. That is how we can meet our ultimate responsibility, and that is to turn over to the next generation a republic in better shape than we received it.

In our resilience, there is more work to be done, and we can do it; we are doing it, for our system of American values has set the foundation, but to move forward, we—all of us—must take off Sambos Glasses to realize the promise of American diversity.

SONG 6

The Promise of American Diversity for the 21ˢᵗ Century

Lives are changed when people are connected.

—Unknown person from the current 2020 protest movement

Traditionally, American culture has been viewed as a melting pot, a homogeneous, relative White society, yet fortunately, the impending American demographic transformation that is taking place currently, as is being reported by the United States Census Bureau, projects that significant socioeconomic and political implications for traditional America have resulted in racial and ethnic minorities accounting for an 83 percent increase in America's population growth in the last decade.

This means that by the year 2050, the United States, for the first time in its history, will be a majority-minority population, with all of America's diversity. The current American house that has been built for Whites, that is about to change, and the transformational nature of the change promises to be good for all of American society.

Dr. Roosevelt Thomas addresses the homogeneous nature of the American house in his fable about a giraffe and the elephant, and the fable goes like this: "A giraffe and an elephant consider themselves as friends. But when the giraffe invites the elephant into his home, disaster strikes. The house has been designed to meet the needs of the tall and slender giraffe. The elephant smashes into doorways and walls, trying to maneuver within the giraffe's home. The giraffe kindly and gently suggests aerobics or ballet classes for the elephant. The elephant is unconvinced. To him, the house is the problem, or as the elephant comments in the metaphor, the homogeneous nature of the house was not built for all of America's diversity."

This transformational change that is taking place could very well begin to build a house that includes all of American's diversity, not just a small segment of the population, yet it will not, nor should it not, transform America into a postracial society.

So what is a postracial society?

President Barack Obama's election has been termed historic by many, including Bettina L. Love and Brandelyn Tosolt, both assistant professors at Northern Kentucky University and who have studied President Obama and the notion of an American postracial society. Professors Tosolt and Love have concluded that though there was a dominant discourse that Obama's election proved the end of American racism, they contend that Obama's election reveals less about the end of racism and more about the public's view of racism as a changing construct. They further contend that the current dissonance may be resolved by entering a postracial period; however, they argue that continued inequities reveal this to be rhetoric rather than reality.

Cornell Belcher at Harvard contends that "the rise of Donald Trump was a predictable backlash. The election of the nation's first Black president does not mean that we live in a postracial society; it means that we are now at a critical historical tipping point demographically and culturally in America, and this tipping point is indeed the wolf at the door for many anxious White Americans."

My concept of the promise of American diversity for the twenty-first century, in concept and in practice, goes beyond the notion of a postracial America, as it explores how American values play out in a more social cohesive America.

The notion of American diversity is set in Dov Seidman framework of situational and sustainable values.

Seidman contends that "relationships, propelled by situational values, involve calculations about what is available in the here and now. They are about exploiting short-term opportunities rather than consistently living the principles that create long-term success. They are all about what we can and cannot do in any given situation."

I contend that leveling Seidman's concept that the promise of American diversity is based on sustainable values and, by contrast, is about what we should and should not do in situations.

As such, it literally sustains relationships over the long term. Such values are the values that connect us deeply as humans, such as transparency, integrity, honesty, truth, shared responsibility, hope, and a sense of community. They are therefore about how, not how much situational values push us toward the strategy of becoming "too big to fail."

Additionally, applying Seidman's concept to the promise of American diversity, sustainable values inspire us to pursue the strategy of becoming too sustainable to fail by building enduring relationships. The promise of diversity addresses this complexity by managing the tension and conflict that tends to go with it.

Furthermore, our political leaders should be responsible for creating a climate of shared values, purpose, and mutual respect among the American citizen and, above all, a common commitment to preserving the very freedoms on which our democracy depends.

Within this frame, citizens should exercise their right to debate how to define the public interest, how to identify the central problems, and how to choose among competing interest; this should be part of embracing my and Seidman's shared concept.

Such debates can be bitter, but our democracy's health depends on our ability, the American citizen, to hold our passions against each other in check and to offer each other at least some benefit of the doubt.

With issues as profoundly complex and sensitive as diversity in society and within our organizations and institutions, I predict that given the results of my applied research, the promise of American diversity will unleash greater levels of creativity, personal adaptability, expanded styles of thinking, and the rendering of public policy, which will lead to a sustainable American community.

So I pose the following:

- When the facts change, what is to be done?
- How confident are you in the truth of your initial beliefs?
- How should you modify your beliefs in the light of new information?
- Do you cling to old assumptions or cultural stereotypes?

The definition of American diversity reflects the all-important individual similarities and differences that each of us brings to any situation.

American diversity represents the historical evolution of the enslavement of the African American, which began in 1619, yet it goes beyond, and as such, has its premise in the concept of sustainable values. Values that comprise the first three lines of Abraham Lincoln's Gettysburg Address: "Fourscore and seven years ago, our fathers brought forth on this continent, a new nation, conceived in liberty, and dedicated to the proposition that all men, now women, are created equal."

American diversity has the following principles:

- It is not an unfortunate by-product of immigration, birth rates, race, and gender issues.
- It builds sustainable communities.
- It builds sustainable competitive organizations.
- It unleashes greater levels of creativity and innovation.
- Applied research supports that it strengthens the problem-solving and decision-making process within communities, organizations, and institutions.

The functional definition of *American diversity* is that of the enslavement of the African American experience of 1619 yet goes beyond to be an inclusive celebration of all of America's similarities and differences.

I would suggest that based on the application of the principles of American diversity, more than ten years of conducting applied research within the United States, and given the range of complex issues that confront the country currently, the following represents five major issues that the promise of American diversity will address:

1. The application of the definition and process would build more respectful interactive personal and professional relationships that are based on the understanding of individual similarities and differences are not a negative but are a positive.

2. The application of the definition and process would build more human sustainable communities that are based on the understanding of individual similarities and differences are not a negative but are a positive.

3. The application of the definition and process would build more sustainable competitive organizations based on applied research that diversity in teams outperforms other workplace constructs.

4. The application of the definition and process would unleash greater levels of creativity and innovation within most sectors of society.

5. The application of the definition and process that America's diversity would be celebrated for its shared and sustainable value within most sectors of society.

American diversity is no longer the process for doing the right thing; it is now the process for doing the essential thing.

SONG 7

Drift and Mastery

The year of 2020 has made us unsettled to the very core of our being.

DEFINITIONS AND TERMS

American diversity: Reflects individual and unique similarities and differences that are within the American context of slavery and the enslavement of the African American experience.

Diversity: Reflects the differences and similarities and related tensions and complexities that can characterize mixtures of any kind. When one speaks of diversity, one is describing a characteristic of a collection or mixture of some kind.

Diversity tension: Reflects the stress and strain that come from the interaction and clashing of differences and similarities.

Diversity complexity: Reflects that which makes something difficult to explain within the diversity context.

Diversity management: Reflects the ability to make quality decisions in the midst of any set of differences and similarities and related tensions and complexities.

BIBLIOGRAPHY

Baldwin, James. "Letter from a Region In My Mind." *The New Yorker* (November 17, 1962).

Brooks, David. *The Road to Character*. Random House, 2015.

Brewster, Todd. *Lincoln's Gamble*. New York, NY 10020: Scribner, A Division of Simon & Schuster Inc., 2014.

Bourguignon, Francois, The Globalization of Inequality, Princeton University Press, 2015.

Coates, Ta-Nehisi. *Between the World and Me*. Spiegel & Grau, 2015.

Comey, James. *A Higher Loyalty: Truth, Lies, and Leadership*. Flatiron Books, 2018.

Charlton, Lauretta. "Race/Related," *The New York Times* (Saturday, August 17, 2019).

Chanlat, Jean-Francois, and Mustafa F. Ozbligin. "Management and Diversity: Thematic Approaches." In *International Perspectives on Equality, Diversity, and Inclusion, Volume 4*. Emerald Publishing, 2017.

Declaration of Independence (1776), except transcript in Congress (July 4, 1776). www.ourdocuments.gov.

DiTomaso, Nancy. *The American Non-Dilemma: Racial Inequality Without Racism.* The Russell Sage Foundation, 2013.

Dyson, Michael Eric. *The Black Presidency.* Houghton Mifflin Harcourt, 2016.

Capehart, Jonathan. *Washington Post* (June 6, 2016): 2.

Coates, Ta-Nehisi. "The Case For Reparations." *The Atlantic*: 71.

Gest, Justin. *The New Minority: White Working Class Politics in an Age of Immigration and Inequality.* Jonathan Capehart, June 6, 2016.

Gross, Ariela, and Alejandro de la Fuente. *The History of Slavery Remains with Us Today.* March 9, 2020.

Haass, Richard. *A World in Disarray: American Foreign Policy and the Crisis of the Old Order.* Penguin Press, 2017.

Hannah-Jones, Nikole. "The 1619 Project." *The New York Times Magazine* (August 18, 2019).

Hughes, Langston. *The Ways of White Folks.* Vintage Classics, Vintage Books, 1990.

Hurston, Zora Neale. "Barracoon: The Story of the Last 'Black Cargo.'" *Amistad* (2018).

Johnson, Lyndon B. Commencement Address at Howard University: "To Fulfill These Rights." June 4, 1965.

Mandela, Nelson. *Long Walk to Freedom.* Little, Brown and Company, 1994.

Marley, Bob. "Redemption Song." September 8, 2009. Inspired by his song, "Redemption Song."

Mitchell, Richard, Marvin L. Winitsky, JD, PhD, and Robert Lattimer. *Sambo Glasses*. January 1981.

Meacham, Jon. *The Soul of America: The Battle for Our Better Angels*. Random House, 2018.

Painter, Nell Irvin. *The History of White People*. W. W. Norton & Company Inc., 2010.

Pew Research Center. "Social & Demographic Trends; Race in America 2019." April 9, 2019.

Peck, Don. Pinched: *How the Great Recession Has Narrowed Our Futures & What We Can Do About It*. New York: CROOWN Publishers Group, 2011.

Smith, Zadie. *Darryl Pinckney's Intimate Study of Black History*.

Taksa, Lucy. *How War Metaphors Can Trigger Racism*. 2019.

West, Cornel. *Race Matters*. Beacon Press, 1993.

Wilson, Valerie, and William Rodgers III. "Black-White Wage Gaps Expand with Rising Wage Inequality." *Economic Policy Institute* (September 20, 2016).

Wilkerson, Isabel. *The Warmth of Other Suns*. Vintage Books, 2010.

Woodward, Bob. *Fear: Trump in the White House*. Simon & Schuster, 2018.

O'Toole, Fintan. "The World Has Loved, Hated and Envied the US. Now, for the First Time, We Pity It." *Irish Times* (April 25, 2020).

Reid, Joy-Ann. *The Man Who Sold America.* William Morrow, an Imprint of HarperCollins Publishers, 2019.

Roosevelt, Thomas R., Jr. *Beyond Race and Gender: Unleashing the Power of Your Total Workforce by Managing Diversity.* AMACOM, 1991.

Stiglitz, Joseph E. *The Great Divide: Unequal Societies and What We Can Do About Them.* W. W. Norton & Company Inc., 2015

Roosevelt, Thomas R., Jr. *Building a House for Diversity.* AMACOM, 1999.

Roosevelt, Thomas R., Jr. *World Class Diversity Management: A Strategic Approach.* Berrett-Koehler Publishers Inc., 2010.

Troutt, David Dante. *The Price of Paradise: The Costs of Inequality and a Vision for a More Equitable America.* New York University Press, 2013.

"The America We Need." *The New York Times.* Opinion, by the Editorial Board (April 9, 2020).

ABOUT THE AUTHOR

Robert L. Lattimer is the nonresident scholar for diversity studies at the John J. Heldrich Center for Workforce Development and a lecturer of public policy at the Edward J. Bloustein School of Planning and Public Policy, at Rutgers, the State University of New Jersey.

Robert is also a visiting professor and serves as an associate member of the Centre for Workforce Futures, within the faculty of Business and Economics, at Macquarie University—Sydney, Australia.

Robert is the published author of more than twenty-four articles that have been published in peer review journals and two book chapters that address the issue of diversity, organizational strategy, and global competitiveness. His diversity research helped shape United States Public Policy in higher education pertaining to the Supreme Court of the United States of America, Barbara Grutter V. Lee Bollinger, the Board of Regents of the University of Michigan, at which the court affirmed diversity as the nation's law in higher education by a decision of five of the nine justices of the court; Robert was listed as an authority of the court.

Robert was appointed by the deputy president of the Republic of South Africa as the lead consultant to assist the national leadership public service with its transformation plans during the period of President Nelson Mandela, working directly with Maxwell Tamsanqua Maisela period covering April 1996 to 2001.

Prior to serving in higher education, Robert was a partner at Andersen/Accenture Consulting performing within the firms Organization & Change Strategy Practice and as a global practice leader at Towers Perrin Consulting, where he led the firms highly successful Diversity Consulting Practice.

Robert also served his country as a combat Marine, being awarded two Purple Hearts and the Bronze Star medal with the Combat "V" as well as being cited as One of The Ten Outstanding Young-men of America with former Vice President of the United States Albert Gore Junior.

Robert's international travel involves France, Australia, Ireland, India, Sri Lanka, Republic of South Africa, Namibia, Canada, Taiwan, and the United Kingdom, where he performs as a consultant, visiting professor, lecturer, and keynote speaker and examines the economic and management processes.